BBC MUSIC

MONTEVERDI CH

D0825258

Bach Cantatas J. A. WESTRUP
Bach Organ Music PETER WILLIAMS
Bartók Chamber Music STEPHEN WALSH
Bartók Orchestral Music JOHN MCCABE
Beethoven Concertos and Overtures ROGER FISKE
Beethoven Piano Sonatas DENIS MATTHEWS
Beethoven String Quartets BASIL LAM
Beethoven Symphonies ROBERT SIMPSON
Berlioz Orchestral Music HUGH MACDONALD
Brahms Chamber Music IVOR KEYS
Brahms Piano Music DENIS MATTHEWS
Brahms Orchestral Music JOHN HORTON
Brahms Songs ERIC SAMS
Bruckner Symphonies PHILIP BARFORD
Couperin DAVID TUNLEY
Debussy Orchestral Music DAVID COX
Debussy Piano Music FRANK DAWES
Dvořák Symphonies and Concertos ROBERT LAYTON
Elgar Orchestral Music MICHAEL KENNEDY
Falla RONALD CRICHTON
Handel Concertos STANLEY SADIE
Haydn String Quartets ROSEMARY HUGHES
Haydn Symphonies H. C. ROBBINS LANDON
Mahler Symphonies and Songs PHILIP BARFORD
Mendelssohn Chamber Music JOHN HORTON
Monteverdi Madrigals DENIS ARNOLD
Mozart Chamber Music A. HYATT KING
Mozart Piano Concertos PHILIP RADCLIFFE
Mozart Serenades, Divertimenti and Dances ERIK SMITH
Mozart Wind and String Concertos A. HYATT KING
Purcell ARTHUR HUTCHINGS
Rachmaninov Orchestral Music PATRICK PIGGOTT
Ravel Orchestral Music LAURENCE DAVIES
Schoenberg Chamber Music ARNOLD WHITTALL
Schubert Chamber Music J. A. WESTRUP
Schubert Piano Sonatas PHILIP RADCLIFFE
Schubert Songs MAURICE J. E. BROWN
Schubert Symphonies MAURICE J. E. BROWN
Schumann Orchestral Music HANS GAL
Schumann Piano Music JOAN CHISSELL
Schumann Songs ASTRA DESMOND
Shostakovich Symphonies HUGH OTTAWAY
Tchaikovsky Ballet Music JOHN WARRACK
Tchaikovsky Symphonies and Concertos JOHN WARRACK
The Trio Sonata CHRISTOPHER HOGWOOD
Vaughan Williams Symphonies HUGH OTTAWAY
Vivaldi MICHAEL TALBOT
Hugo Wolf Songs MOSCO CARNER

BBC MUSIC GUIDES

Monteverdi Church Music

DENIS ARNOLD

BRITISH BROADCASTING CORPORATION

Published by the
British Broadcasting Corporation
35 Marylebone High Street
London W1M 4AA

ISBN 0 563 12884 4

First published 1982

© Denis Arnold 1982

Filmset in Great Britain by
August Filmsetting, Warrington, Cheshire
Printed in England by
Hollen Street Press, Slough, Berkshire

Contents

Introduction

Monteverdi was born and lived in a time of great religious fervour. It was a time of saints: Teresa, Charles Borromeo, Philip Neri – with the memory of Ignatius and Francis Xavier still very alive. It was a time of fine churches: S. Maria in Vallicella and S. Andrea della Valle in Rome and the Redentore in Venice, the Duomo Nuovo at Brescia and S. Barbara at Mantua. It was a time of great church music: Palestrina's mature Mass settings and motet cycle on the *Song of Songs*, Lasso's *Penitential Psalms*, the *Concerti* of Andrea Gabrieli and *Sacrae Symphoniae* of Giovanni Gabrieli. It was, in fact, the time of what we call the Counter-Reformation.

The fervour did not last at the same pitch throughout the whole of Monteverdi's long life. The Council of Trent had completed its deliberations just before his birth in 1567. The signs are that although – for musicians at least – it had a strong immediate effect, by the turn of the century great composers were turning to other things. But there can be no doubt that during Monteverdi's formative years, religious music was at a peak. And Palestrina's fine Mass, *Assumpta est Maria*, shows just as much as the motets of the great Venetians that it had a public face. The Counter-Reformation was not so much a time of quiet devotion but of missionising. The troops of the Jesuit order fought their battles for the influence of princes: the Oratorians of Philip Neri fought for the hearts of men with sermons, hymns and theatrical spectacle. The Church of Rome was determined to use all the power of the senses to show mankind the glory of God: *in majorem Dei et Ecclesiae gloriam* was the motto of Pope Sixtus V in designing a new Rome. Thus its music was often grand and emotional.

The most obvious manifestation of the desire for public grandeur in church music was to be found in Venice. In St Mark's – the Doge's official chapel, the equivalent of London's Westminster Abbey – the *cappella* was large: some twenty-five singers in the choir and up to the same number of instrumentalists for festival days. The style was based on the concept of *cori spezzati*, or divided choirs; groups of choristers were separated in the famous galleries of the basilica, from where they sang in dialogue, as it were, each phrase coming from a different place so as to amaze the listeners in the nave beneath. Cornetts and trombones would reinforce the voices to provide splendid sonorities. Thus were the foreign visitors, ambassadors, princes or rich German merchants impressed with the power of the Most Serene Republic.

Once a fair corpus of this music had been published in 1587 in a large volume called *Concerti*, containing works by the Gabrielis, the fashion spread throughout Italy. The Bologna composers working for the huge basilica of S. Petronio took it up, publishing volumes with similar titles. It was popular not only in Italy: the Germans liked it, too, and a continual stream of composers came from the various northern European courts to study in Venice. Nor was it just a northern find. Palestrina published some equally splendid music for *cori spezzati* as early as 1572. Admittedly the Romans do not seem to have used instruments on the same scale as the Venetians; but voices alone can be impressive if church sonorities are imaginatively exploited. Palestrina, known today as the master of polyphony, in fact in later life was more concerned with music which stupefied the sense of hearing rather than delighted the intellect. Though there is ample imitative counterpoint in such a Mass as the one entitled *Te Deum laudibus*, the main impression on the listener must have been that of the variety of sonority possible from a small six-stranded choir; mighty tenors and basses were matched against brilliant soprano castrati, and its full sound was brilliant at such moments as the opening to the Credo.

Things were not always as rosy as at St Mark's or in the Sistine Chapel. We have the evidence of a *maestro di cappella* (Lodovico Viadana, who had worked at several provincial cathedrals and monastic churches) that motets and Masses were performed with parts missing, simply because the choir was insufficient in numbers (and probably also in skill). Yet the point of interest in the preface to his first book of *Concerti* (1602), where he gives us this information, is precisely that he was concerned to invent a method of composition which would get round this problem. So came into being the *basso continuo*, a notation which allowed the organist to play chords, indicated by a bass line, to accompany just a single singer on occasion – or a very small group if things were a shade more accommodating. The impression we obtain from this and the flood of concertante motets which exploited this invention is that music had come to be considered desirable in many a small church where previously there had been none. The new manner was quickly picked up by organists and choirmasters who had not (and perhaps could not have) mastered the old contrapuntal idiom. With this new style, anyone who could write some simple melody and back it up with elementary chords could claim to be a composer – and many did. But alongside these amateurs there were real composers who saw the possibilities opened up by a style based on attractive and expressive melody supported by perhaps a simple, though not to be despised harmonic, idiom.

The best of these composers achieved passion: for the non-public face of the Counter-Reformation is the individual's profound religious feeling. Even before the *basso continuo* became popular, there had been this side to church music. As early as the 1560s, Lasso had composed some deeply-felt chromatic motets, in which the chromatic harmonies developed in that secret art, the *musica reservata* of Munich, were used. There is often a strong sense of sin in such motets, the prevailing mood being one of terror, as in the setting of *Timor et tremor* in which the trembling is caused by the thought of eternal damnation – the same state of mind that is induced in the early stages of the Jesuit *Spiritual Exercises* where the exercitant must 'see the flames of Hell, smell the sulphur and stench, hear the shrieks of the sufferers, taste the bitterness of their tears and feel their remorse'.[1]

Just as later in these *Spiritual Exercises* the participant evokes the Ascension of Christ, so does other music find the joys of religion. Here the motets for solo voice or voice with organ accompaniment often express such contentment by analogy with earthly love, motets to the Blessed Virgin being written in an erotic idiom derived from the secular song books of the time. Some of Monteverdi's colleagues were excellent in this manner, notably his assistant in St Mark's, Alessandro Grandi, whose settings of parts of the *Song of Songs*, a favourite hunting ground for the musician seeking texts throughout the Counter-Reformation period, are indeed luscious and erotic. Such works show the human face of the movement, just as clearly as do the New Testament scenes of Caravaggio or the martyrological statues of Bernini.

This, then, is the age of Monteverdi, and if many will prefer the religious music of the earlier Renaissance found in the balance of Josquin, or the more theological approach of the later Baroque conveyed in the patterned art of the Protestant J. S. Bach, there can be no doubt of the power of the church music of this time. Though the historians of music have usually concentrated on the secular

[1] R. Wittkower, *Art and Architecture in Italy 1600-1750* (London, 1958).

genres — opera, monody — of the time and found church music less exciting and in the rearguard of musical advance, it is doubtful whether anybody saw it that way at the time. Opera was a delight for the rich connoisseurs, a thing for royal weddings and celebrations; monodic song sought a numerically wider but socially no less restricted audience. Church music was all around everyone. Italians do not divide their lives into secular and religious areas as northerners frequently do. Monteverdi, significantly, when classifying music did not write about 'secular' and 'sacred', but about two 'practices' which obeyed different aesthetic principles, according to the composer's attitude to setting words. To think, as some commentators have done, of his church music as 'secular' in tone is to misunderstand his mentality. Just as an anti-clerical Italian communist will seek the comfort of his priest when *in extremis*, so Monteverdi takes church music for granted. When he was bidden to compose it, he did so to the fullness of his capacity, just as he did an opera or madrigal when that duty called. And being a great composer, he naturally composed some great masterpieces in all these forms.

Youth at Cremona

Claudio Monteverdi was born at Cremona, the eldest child of a chemist who, in the manner of his time, also practised medicine in a modest (and, strictly speaking, illegal) way. Cremona, in the realm of the Dukes of Milan, was — and remains — a provincial town without great pretensions to a musical life, not perhaps too dissimilar to the Worcester of the young Edward Elgar, though lacking the stimulus which the *Three Choirs Festival* gave that city. But as at Worcester, the musical life was effectively organised around the cathedral and its director of music. During Monteverdi's early years this was Marc' Antonio Ingegneri, a reasonably well-known composer, many of whose works were issued by the great publishing houses of Gardano and Amadino in Venice. Since Monteverdi's father had his shop near the square in the heart of Cremona, it is very likely that he met Ingegneri; and having two musical sons, he put them to study with him.

In later life, Monteverdi was to include Ingegneri amongst the moderns, the composers of that 'second practice' exemplified in

Monteverdi's own revolutionary madrigals. All that one can say of this is that it is hard to see why. Perhaps it was because Ingegneri did in places use various chromatic harmonies which were somewhat unusual in the 1570s when the madrigals containing them were published. Perhaps it was that Ingegneri talked to the lad about the humanistic principles of word-setting then current, introducing Monteverdi to concepts which were to dominate his work for most of his lifetime. But in fact Ingegneri was a conservative, a sound contrapuntist and competent composer of church music in the traditional style. It is interesting that he wrote some Holy Week music, the *Improperia* (once ascribed to Palestrina), which uses the technique of chordal chanting known as *falsobordone*, for his pupil's famous Vespers music published in 1610 was to use the same device. In the main, however, his music shows a mastery of counterpoint, which he passed on to Monteverdi.

Monteverdi's textbook was probably Zarlino's *Le Istitutioni Harmoniche*,[1] an enormous treatise published in 1558 which contains a great deal of speculative writing about the attitude of the Ancient Greeks to music. But it also gives some down-to-earth and extremely useful instructions on how to write solid Netherlandish counterpoint, starting in the usual way by adding parts to a cantus firmus, or melody, often derived from plainsong, in long notes (another technique which will reappear in the Vespers). There are signs that Ingegneri also encouraged another method of learning the trade, the imitating or 'parodying' of existing compositions, using similar themes and harmonic ideas while developing them somewhat differently.

Monteverdi's first publication came out in 1582, when the composer was fifteen. The publisher was the famous house of Gardano in Venice, the dedicatee a priest, the title-page making clear that 'Claudini Montisviridi' was a disciple of Ingegneri; all of which adds up to the fact that the boy was being well promoted by somebody. The title *Sacrae Cantiunculae* implies a volume of motets, common enough for an incipient church musician – but the fact that they are written for three voices was unusual for the 1580s, a time when bigger forces were preferred to provide a great sonority. The genre had been more popular thirty years earlier, and some phrases similar to those in some of the Roman composer Costanzo Festa's

[1] Monteverdi's copy has survived, though it is possible he acquired it later in life.

three-voiced motets published in the 1540s suggest that Ingegneri had directed Monteverdi's attention to this by now somewhat 'dated' music.

That the volume is something of a manifesto is indicated by the relatively impractical nature of many of the motets. While some could be sung by two counter-tenors and tenor, others seem to need a choir with boys – and boys' choirs were more a Netherlands institution than an Italian one. But it is their manner which convinces us that many of them were meant to show off youthful prowess. Each phrase will be stated by a single voice, then imitated by the other two, and such imitative treatment is rarely leavened by chordal textures. There is nothing wrong with this in short works of this kind: yet the more experienced Roman composers of the mid-century used a greater variety of means. Festa, for example, after beginning a motet to a text from the *Song of Songs*, *'Quam pulchra es'*, in just this way, has a magical passage in which the upper voices seem to call to each other 'veni, veni dilecta mea' – 'come, come my beloved' – in a way most expressive of the words.

Ex.1 *Quam pulchra es* (Festa)

Monteverdi cannot match this, though there is some neat word painting when in *O Domine Jesu Christe* keen dissonances tell of the agony on the Cross.

Ex.2 *O Domine Jesu Christe*

In general, however, Monteverdi works out a series of well-established clichés which allow for easy imitation throughout the parts, often based on scale passages which are smooth and singable. Rhythms are smooth also: there is little syncopation and hence little excitement, even when he breaks into triple time, which the Gabrielis put to brilliant use in their 'alleluia' refrains. Just occasionally there is a more imaginative touch and, significantly, these generally occur when Monteverdi is inspired by the words. The spouse in the *Song of Songs* is bidden to arise and come to her lover. The opening word suggests a cluster of rising quick notes in *Surge propera*.

Ex.3 *Surge propera*

Equally, the image of Christ standing up among his disciples and blessing them produces some lively writing in *Surgens Jesus*. Already Monteverdi was sensitive to the pictorial elements in a text, a pointer to the future.

The real reason why the *Sacrae Cantiunculae* seem student work is nevertheless more connected by their lack of well-considered proportions. Looking at the three-voiced motets of Lasso first published in the 1570s shows a composer who works out the thematic material of each phrase thoroughly and consistently. In a piece such as *Diligam te Domine* he divides a short text into four or five phrases each of which then is developed for eight or ten bars, the first one at still greater length to build up a climax. In *Beati omnes* the text is longer, so some phrases are set as duets – but here, too, nothing seems skimped. Monteverdi is more casual. If he alights on a musical phrase which will develop fluently, so be it: but if the phrase is not so happily invented, it is likely to be brushed aside quite quickly. Then there is the matter of continuity. The difficulty of writing for only three voices is that if one of them is rested for any length of time, the sound seems thin. Lasso gets round this either by writing a duet which is conceived as music for two voices (that is, the rhythms interlock and there is little use of imitation) or by resting each voice in turn for a very short breathing space. Monteverdi more often keeps all the voices continuously employed, which makes both for breathlessness and a certain monotony of sound. When he seemingly embarks on a duet (as in the extract from *Surge propera* quoted in Ex. 3) it frequently turns out to be a trio lacking one voice, a fact revealed by the eventual entry of the missing voice with the theme, which may by then have exhausted its momentum. So is technical inexperience revealed.

Nevertheless, this is just inexperience. Some German scholars, liking to make contrasts between northern and southern music, have suggested that Monteverdi, an Italian 'colourist' with a natural flair for creating sonorities, was never at home composing contrapuntally in the traditions of the Netherlands or Germany. But this antithesis of north and south is an oversimplification of both national and historical trends. Monteverdi was tackling a difficult medium in these three-voiced motets. It is harder to compose for three than for four performers, as is shown by the paucity of satisfactory string trios compared to the number of string quartets. Clearly this 'disciple of Ingegneri' had been set to work at mastering contrapuntal techniques, and although the boy of fifteen had not yet achieved such mastery, the grown man was to do so. We may therefore not grieve if the *Sacrae Cantiunculae* are not great music, nor feel guilty at not performing more than one or two of them. The fruits of this early study will soon be revealed.

The Mantuan Vespers

But not too soon. In the event, his compositional training with the cathedral choirmaster was to further directly neither Monteverdi's immediate career nor his subsequent fame. He gained his first job as a string player in the household of the Gonzagas at Mantua; which probably meant that he joined an ensemble used mainly for dance music, a Jewish dancing master being part of the establishment. Fame was to come from his madrigals,[1] in which he quickly showed his appreciation of the fashionable humanist thinking concerning the uses of words and music held necessary in leading to that ideal aim of *muovere gli affetti* or 'moving the whole man' so greatly advocated and admired by the Greek philosophers. Seemingly his duties did not as yet include the composition of church music, which was well looked after in his earliest Mantua years by Monteverdi's hero, Giaches de Wert, in overall charge of both chamber and chapel music at the Gonzaga court, and also the *maestro di cappella* in the Ducal Chapel of S. Barbara, Giovanni Giacomo Gastoldi, known to history for his balletti (or dance songs) which were imitated – indeed purloined – by Thomas Morley, but who was a very efficient composer of church music also. On Wert's death Benedetto Pallavicino took on some of the burden, and although Monteverdi tended to despise him, he too was no mean composer.

Monteverdi learned much from these men and not only from their secular music. He must have taken part in the performance of the Masses, psalm settings and motets. These left their mark on his own church music. The Mantuan taste in church music can be traced in various ways. The library of the basilica of S. Barbara (the ducal chapel), still preserved – at least in part – in Milan, shows that the dukes liked the old-fashioned polyphonic music of the Nether-

[1] See Denis Arnold's *Monteverdi Madrigals* in the BBC Music Guides Series (London, 1967).

landers. Old Duke Guglielmo, who had set up the basilica between 1562 and 1565, also liked the *alternim* style, in which some sections of the Mass were sung in plainsong, others in full choral polyphony; he commissioned several settings from no less a master than Palestrina. Venetian polychoral music, the Gabrielian style of writing for separated choirs - *cori spezzati* - was not unknown either, as some of Pallavicino's motets show. Then there was *falsobordone*, or the chordal chanting of the words of the psalms (not unlike Anglican chant in effect, if rather different in detail), with the end of each section given a more elaborate polyphonic cadence; Gastoldi was an expert in this. But we may suspect that Monteverdi's heart really went out to the motet manner of Wert, whereby the deeply emotional style of the *fin-de-siècle* madrigal was adapted so as to turn chamber music into something grander, more suitable for choirs. Here the modern means - of chromaticism, of the sharply chiselled motif which was so easily memorable, and above all of the attempt to match the detail of the words by expressive music - were not excluded.

Experience of this music was to stand him in good stead when, on the death of Pallavicino in 1601, Monteverdi applied to the Duke 'most humbly to become director of music in your chamber and chapel'. Monteverdi, still only thirty-four, was granted his request and presumably now could be called on to compose in any genre, either secular or sacred. How much church music he had to compose in the next few years is unknown: probably not a great deal, since Gastoldi was still in charge at S. Barbara. More likely Monteverdi would have provided music for special occasions and, being known as an operatic composer, the motet for solo voice or for small ensemble soon became his *métier*. It would not be surprising if those motets of this nature published in his Vespers music volume of 1610, his first collection of church music since the *Sacrae Cantiunculae*, were not composed from time to time during the first decade of the century.

Perhaps he was also expected to compose church music for grander occasions. Certainly the big psalm settings and settings of the *Magnificat* of this 1610 volume seem to have been written for such an event, demanding highly skilled forces and - knowing Monteverdi's habits with other large-scale works - ample rehearsal. If performed in full, there is a need for an extensive instrumental ensemble, and it is this that has led one scholar to speculate whether the occasion was a Sunday during the famous opera festival of 1608.[1] To celebrate the marriage of the heir apparent, Prince Francesco Gonzaga, to the Infanta Margherita of Savoy a new order of knighthood was inaugurated on that day with the service of Vespers in the huge church of S. Andrea. Certainly, if the now lost opera *L'Arianna* was scored for the same type of ensemble as the previous year's *L'Orfeo*, the orchestra could have been deployed for the Vespers – and indeed the vocal ensemble, which included castrati among a group of fine soloists, would have fitted the bill equally well.

Be that as it may, there can be little doubt that the psalm settings, hymn, and settings of the *Magnificat* were composed as a unity, for they all use similar techniques: '*composta sopra canti fermi*', as the title-page of the 1610 publication has it. Although it is possible to perform any one, or group of them, independently, they do hang together better as a liturgical entity. When they came to be published, Monteverdi did a remarkable thing. Instead of printing them one after the other in the usual way, he interspersed the various motets for solo voice already mentioned, separating the psalms as if by antiphons – though the motets do not set liturgical antiphon texts. Why did he do this? No one knows: but anyone who assumes that Monteverdi did this accidentally should know better. Monteverdi was a careful and thoughtful composer who did not easily break with convention. Present-day experience also teaches that to perform the separate items in Monteverdi's printed order makes good sense. There is feeling for natural climax in the way that the motets begin with a solo, then add a duet, next a duet which develops into a trio, and conclude with an echo piece using all six voices of the ensemble.

By this time, Monteverdi was very interested in making his large-scale works totally unified. In a later letter, he describes how his operas *L'Orfeo* and *L'Arianna* had real climaxes: the one is Orpheus' song to the boatman to ferry him to Hades, the other is the famous 'Lament' of the heroine. It is not too fanciful to see the same kind of planning in the Vespers. In saying this, it must be said that the volume includes in fact two settings of the Vespers music in one: one using a massive (by the standards of the time) instrumental ensemble, the other for voices alone. That using instruments is the more complete, though the alternative is not to be despised. We may list these alternatives as follows:

[1] I. Fenlon, 'The Monteverdi Vespers – suggested answers to some fundamental questions', *Early Music*, V (1977) pp. 380-7.

	'Full' Vespers	'Little' Vespers
Versicle and Responses:	*Deus in adjutorium* for 6 voices and 6 instruments	*Deus in adjutorium* for 6 voices in the manner of a *falsobordone*
Psalm:	*Dixit Dominus*, 6 vv. and 6 instruments	*Dixit Dominus,* 6 vv. omitting ritornellos
Motet:	*Nigra sum*, 1 v. and *basso continuo*	*Nigra sum*, 1 v. and *basso continuo*
Psalm:	*Laudate pueri*, 8 vv. and *basso continuo*	*Laudate pueri*, 8 vv. and *basso continuo*
Motet:	*Pulchra es*, 2 vv. and *basso continuo*	*Pulchra es*, 2 vv. and *basso continuo*
Psalm:	*Laetatus sum*, 6 vv. and *basso continuo*	*Laetatus sum*, 6 vv. and *basso continuo*
Motet:	*Duo seraphim*, 3 vv. and *basso continuo*	*Duo seraphim*, 3 vv. and *basso continuo*
Psalm:	*Nisi Dominus*, 10 vv. in 2 choirs	*Nisi Dominus*, 10 vv. in 2 choirs
Motet:	*Audi, coelum*, echo piece, 6 vv. and *basso continuo*	*Audi, coelum*, echo piece, 6 vv. and *basso continuo*
Psalm:	*Lauda Jerusalem*, 7 vv. and *basso continuo*	*Lauda Jerusalem*, 7 vv. and *basso continuo*
Sonata sopra	*Sancta Maria* for 1 v.	
Hymn:	*Ave maris stella*, 8 vv. and 5 instruments	*Ave maris stella*, 8 vv. omitting ritornello
Magnificat I:	7 vv., 6 instruments	*Magnificat* II, 6 vv. and *basso continuo*

Thus, although this Vespers music is very suitable for a large festival when a grand instrumental group is available, it is also possible where there is only a choir and organist. The choir in any case will have to be a good one, with some excellent solo voices; though it may be noticed in passing that it does not have to be large, and that the work could be sung by a largish consort of ten voices (this is needed for *Nisi Dominus*) even if it goes better with a few more (it would become very tiring if there was only one voice to each part throughout the whole). But if the Vespers is sung by a small group the necessity to agree on the alternation between so-called 'choirs' and soloists – which has taken up the time and energy of several editors – tends to disappear, as the sound is not so dissimilar. The choir or consort, it must be said, is differently constituted from the conventional English cathedral choir. There is little evidence that boys were used to sing the upper lines, ample evidence that these were taken by castratos or falsettists. In the larger-scale version, it may be assumed that the instruments frequently doubled the voices even when the music is not so marked. On the other hand, the need to change the colour scheme of the accompanying instrumental group from time to time has never been proved; and if, say, a violin or cornett is added to the basic vocal line, there is no reason to assume that it does not play throughout the piece – just as the voice sings the whole melodic strand. Nor has it been proved that there is a great need for much additional elaborate ornamentation: Monteverdi seems to have written as much as he wanted (as indeed he did in his early operas and madrigals). The work is in fact much more straightforward than modern editions sometimes would have us believe. Sung in the tradition of sixteenth-century polyphony, without heavy accents and with a flowing sense of rhythm, Monteverdi's notes need comparatively few changes or additions.

Common to each version are the settings of the five psalms which are central to the Office of Vespers. As we shall see, the other major sung piece, the *Magnificat*, is set twice, though the two settings are very alike in many ways. The solo motets are equally usable with or without the instrumental ensemble. Admittedly, the opening versicle, *Deus in adjutorium*, is drastically altered without instruments, to the point of being a different piece; on the other hand, the omission of the ritornellos from the hymn *Ave maris stella*, although a pity, does not really change its nature. The omission of the sonata, however desirable the piece is when the instruments are used to maintain a continuity (and perhaps even to justify their presence), does no liturgical damage and musically is no more harmful than the lack of an organ voluntary in an Anglican service. Thus although Monteverdi's Vespers, as it is commonly known today, seems too opulently conceived for ordinary use in church, it is clearly based on liturgical practice.

Monteverdi's interest in musical unity is seen at its clearest in the settings of the psalms and those of the *Magnificat*. The title-page's gloss, '*composta sopra canti fermi*', simply means that each piece uses plainsong material in some way. This was very unusual in the early seventeenth century and one is hard put to find anything remotely similar by any other composer of the period. On the other hand, in the previous century such a usage had not been too uncommon, there having existed at that time two major attitudes to plainsong.

The first was to use it as a structural device, with one part (say the tenors) singing the chant in long held notes, while the other voices added elaborate contrapuntal lines which might or might not be related thematically to the chant. The other way was what is frequently known today as a 'paraphrase' technique, whereby the phrases of plainsong are given distinctive rhythms and are used in imitative counterpoint as though they had been totally invented by the composer. Palestrina used both manners, the 'held note' one mainly in his early works, the 'paraphrase' one in many later pieces, where the nature of plainsong helps to give his music a smoothness and feeling of singability which composers using totally original material rarely equal. Monteverdi also uses both in the psalms of his Vespers: but perhaps understanding of his techniques comes best by placing the psalms in the context of the whole work.

The opening *Deus in adjutorium* is literally an overture – that to Monteverdi's own opera, *L' Orfeo*, to which voices chanting the words of the response on a single chord are added. The overture is a fanfare or toccata (Shakespeare's 'tucket') played by all the instruments in D major three times to warn the audience that the opera was beginning. Here it is also played in D major three times to the choral chant, but there are differences. In between each 'verse' of the text (and thus repetition of the fanfare) the instruments play a short dance-like ritornello; and at the end this is developed into a grand coda to the word 'alleluia'. Nevertheless, its intention to act as overture is clear.

Then comes the first psalm, *Dixit Dominus*; not one of the longest psalm texts, but nonetheless ample enough to require thought about its construction. Psalms are constructed in verses: Monteverdi therefore constructs his music in equivalent sections, each with its own texture. The opening, 'Dixit Dominus Domino meo', uses the plainsong paraphrase developing the theme polyphonically until it is brought to a tutti. The next section, the 'Sede a dextris meis, Donec ponam inimicos tuos, scabellum pedum tuorum', is a *falsobordone*, the words alternately chanted in chords, then flowing with more elaborate cadential counterpoint, this spilling over into a brief instrumental interlude. In 'Virgam virtutis' the plainsong is now deployed in long notes – but as a bass played by the organ, while two sopranos and a bass sing a trio about it in the manner of a madrigal. These techniques – paraphrase, long note cantus firmus and *falsobordone* – take up the rest of the piece, giving a large amount of variety to the sound. But perhaps even more important than its structure is the way that the words are vividly painted, the Lord as Judge being conveyed by a trumpet-like phrase (Ex. 4a), which is amplified by thoughts of victory (Ex. 4b overleaf). At the doxology, that timelessness which comes from the continuous declaiming of a chord comes into its own: 'As it was in the beginning, is now and ever shall be' is aptly conveyed, as voice chases voice in close imitations, over an unchanging chord.

Ex.4 *Dixit Dominus*

[The Basso continuo doubles the Bass line]

Ex. 4

(b)

The first motet, *Nigra sum*, is to words taken from the *Song of Songs*, a popular source for such pieces, since its eroticism allows for music originally developed to set the pastoral eroticism of madrigal and opera. 'I am black' sings the tenor soloist in a brooding, lower register: 'but I am comely' provokes repetitions of a more lively motif, complete with decorative figures. 'Rise up, my love, and come away' is expressed first by a rising scale in both voice and bass, then

Ex. 4b (cont.)

by a voluptuous phrase, full of dissonance and passionate declamation. Yet just as Monteverdi seems to be breaking into an operatic love song, he is recalled (paradoxically) to the timelessness of his subject, 'Tempus putationis abiit',[1] and reverts to quasi-plainsong in the voice part, the organ bass measuring time in a steady tread of crotchets.

[1] Song of Solomon, ii. 12, given in A. V. as 'the time of the singing of birds is come', but the literal translation of *putatio* is 'pruning' or 'reckoning'.

The next psalm, *Laudate pueri*, is set for double choir: the scale of the conception is clearly growing. The plainsong is first deployed in paraphrase fashion, leading quickly to a grand climax. But this is no simple expression of rejoicing in the manner of the Venetians when setting a psalm for double choir. Soon the texture is reduced to a series of duets and trios (the plainsong in long notes sometimes acting as anchor). There is also a Baroque delight in sudden contrasts, as when the basses have sung a duet descending low for the words 'et humilia respicit in coelo et in terra' – 'and looketh down on the low things in heaven and on earth' – the tutti pounces in a vividly dashing triple time to say 'Suscitans a terra inopem' – 'Raising up the needy from the earth'. The doxology is less innocent than that of *Dixit Dominus*, grand church sound giving way in the 'Amen' to a 'still small voice' – or rather two, for the end comes with the two tenors finally giving up their wreathing ornaments and fading into nothing.

Pulchra es (Thou art fair) is one of Monteverdi's most honeyed duets. Again the words come from the *Song of Songs*; again the composer feels their eroticism deeply. Monteverdi's preference for duet rather than solo can be felt, for it allows for amplification of the scale. First one soprano will announce a phrase, then it will be repeated with both singers, the second adding delicious detail, especially in filling in dissonances in unexpected places. The prize phrase must surely, though, come at the words 'Averte oculos tuos a me' (Turn away thine eyes from me), first stated simply by the first soprano, then made much more insistent by its division between two, 'a me – a me – a me' (Ex. 5 opposite).

The stately tread of plainsong returns with the next psalm *Laetatus sum* though it is made clear from the beginning that this is no conventional sixteenth-century paraphrase motet, but a concertante piece in which the organ bass controls the harmony by a walking motif first harmonising the tenor's announcement of the theme. The technique is that of a kaleidoscope, the colours and patterns of voices changing, now quite full, now no more than a solo or duet. As time goes on, the melody seems to gather ornaments, at one magical moment all the voices passionately syncopating the word 'propter' over a held bass note in a massive build-up of sound. And this gorgeousness of sonority dominates the doxology, as if in contrast to the mysterious ending of *Laudate pueri*.

The next motet, *Duo seraphim*, is not a mainly erotic piece, as the

Ex.5 *Pulchra es*

others have been, but an evocation of the mystery of the Trinity, the Three-in-One. The opening is full of prolonged ecstatic discords which grow steadily more St Teresa-like and anguished. Only when these angels sing 'sanctus' does any measure of emotional equilibrium return – and then not much, since they continue with their sobbing trills and interlocking embellishment. Things become calmer at the words 'Plena est omnis terra', with regular imitations between the voices and a measure of smoothness in the ornaments. A third angel arrives with 'Tres sunt qui testimonium dant in coelo'; and ecstasy returns, the moment of complete stillness being achieved at the words 'Et hi tres' (embodied on a single major chord) 'unum sunt' (a unison on the voices). With three angels now to praise the Lord, the development is prolonged and satisfying.

Nisi Dominus would be a conventional psalm setting for two choirs if it were not for one major feature and some significant details. The major issue is that it is based on the 'long note' plainsong style, with the melody given to a tenor part in each choir. The details include the very close working of the other melodic strands, with much use of canon at the half beat, the effect of which is to take away the natural ebb and flow of the music provided normally by accent and unaccent, so that there is continually stress. Another detail of some importance is that, come the 'Gloria patri' in the doxology, both choirs sing the same music to increase the weight of sound; while at the 'Sicut erat in principio' Monteverdi literally goes back to the beginning, repeating the music of *Nisi Dominus* to the words. The sound is noticeably unbrilliant: the layout of the choral sound is usually rather low. It is as though Monteverdi is preparing for something more splendid.

Splendour is not the immediate effect of the next and final motet, *Audi, coelum*. This is an echo piece, a favourite device in opera where shepherds seeking their beloved shepherdesses encounter rocks which throw back the name of Phyllis or Chloris; and not unknown in religious music, for the Venetians − though not the most serious Venetians − put echo effects in some of their double choir motets. But surely this is a trick piece − a gimmick we might say today? To which the answer must be 'no': it is perhaps the most sheerly sublime piece in Monteverdi's Vespers. The opening section is in the manner of the solo madrigals recently developed in Florence. The important words are ornamented while the harmony remains still and un- moving, to allow the singer to show off the beauty of his voice. The echoing voice changes the words on each intervention: 'benedicam' becomes 'dicam', 'remedium' becomes 'medium'. Both voices luxuriate on the word 'Maria' where the plea for the Blessed Virgin's intercession becomes very urgent. Then the principal tenor invites everyone to join in the prayer 'Omnes hanc ergo sequamur' and the full ensemble comes in on a huge, sonorous chord, then breaks into vigorous counterpoint. There is a brief interlude for the echoing tenors before the tutti repeats its music to different words. And next comes the miracle. Monteverdi often finds greatest beauty in simplicity. The words 'Benedicta es, virgo Maria' are set to plain melody, plainly harmonised. The resemblance to some of the madrigals to texts from the pastoral play *Il Pastor Fido* is unmistakable: but this is not in the least sacrilegious, just intensely beautiful and moving. When the piece comes to a quiet ending, it is clear that this has been the moment of truth.

Indeed, what is left to express is mainly the exuberance of triumph. The final psalm of the Vespers, *Lauda Jerusalem Dominum*, does just that. The sound is brilliant − indeed the vocal tessituras are higher than those in the other psalms, and there is some ground for thinking that this psalm should be transposed down to fit the ranges persisting throughout the rest of the music. Yet surely it should be brilliant and Monteverdi's present mode of writing it in a high key makes this intention very clear. The forces are just seven voices (doubling by instruments does not really do much to increase the sonority), divided into two groups of three with a single group of tenors singing a rhythmicised version of the plainsong. It is the one piece which puts the Venetian-style dialogue to good effect, the constant alterations between the two opposing groups propelling the music forward. The climax, however, is purely Monteverdian. The technique of making voices follow each other at the half beat produces the same feeling of continual stress that we have noticed in *Nisi Dominus*. It requires absolute concentration on the part of the singers, for with a moment of inattention all is lost. The doxology is splendid and gorgeous, the plainsong now sung in long notes by the soprano, as if to proclaim the variety of the Everlasting Church from the rooftops; but the end comes in closely-argued dialogue, as exciting as ever.

After that, it is difficult to see what can follow. Modern conductors often put an interval there, to rest the performers and relax the audience. At Mantua in the 1600s this can hardly have been possible, though certainly the Office of Vespers does not employ the musician continuously. Monteverdi puts next in his 1610 volume a strange piece, *Sonata sopra Sancta Maria, ora pro nobis*. The basic concept is that of a litany: the voice chants repeated 'Sancta Maria, ora pro nobis' (Holy Mary, pray for us) as if in procession. The idea of surrounding the chant with an instrumental canzona was not unknown either, and a number of minor composers in North Italy had written such works.[1] What is unique is the scale of Monteverdi's conception. His instrumental ensemble is large by the standards of the day: two cornetts to be played by true virtuosos, two violins demanding equal skill, four trombones (or alternatively three plus another stringed instrument) and a continuo player – probably an organist. He begins with an easily memorable theme tossed between cornetts and violins in duple time. He comes to a cadence, then transforms the theme into triple time, as dance composers did with

[1] A canzona was originally a transcription for instruments of a French *chanson*. By 1610 similar pieces without words, written especially for instruments, were popular.

pavans and galliards. He now embarks on a series of dazzling virtuoso passages – first for the violins, then the trombones, then the cornetts – before the whole ensemble is involved, the soprano singing the litany chant. As the rhythms change, so does the chant become less staid and more passionate. 'Sancta Maria' the voice sings, breaking before the plea 'ora pro nobis' in one repetition: 'San-cta – Ma-ria – o-ra, pro nobis' it gasps on another. Finally the opening 'pavan – galliard' returns (canzonas frequently had da capos at this time), the voice added for two final statements of the chant. This *Sonata sopra Sancta Maria* is a puzzling piece both aesthetically (for it is virtuosic rather than emotional) and to perform. The balance between voice and instruments is, at first, strangely awry, and even when each individual line is played just by a single instrument, the vocal part tends to be swamped. To have this sung by a boys' choir, as is often done today, is to impose a German solution on Italian music, for the *Sängerknaben* of German churches were often given the chorales to sing in Lutheran surroundings; this was unknown in Catholic Italy. It may be that a single soprano was stationed in a gallery or on a raised platform some distance away from the instruments (several Italian writers suggest similar dispositions of their forces) – and although this increases the hazards of ensemble, it cuts down those of co-ordination of a choir with an orchestra, as well as preserving the essential madrigalian subtleties in the later repetitions of the chant.

There are no such problems with the hymn *Ave maris stella*, though admittedly it lends itself to enterprising stationing of forces, this soloist placed near the altar, that one in a transept, yet another in a gallery. In fact it is beautiful enough to have no need of such tricks. Hymns are strophic: *Ave maris stella* has seven verses. What is more natural than to set each in a different way? Monteverdi begins with an eight-part setting of the first one, the forces split into two choirs, the plainchant tune given in a delicious paraphrase to the sopranos of the first choir. The second verse changes the tune into triple time with delicate hemiolas or changes of accent: 1-2-3, 1-2-3, 1-2, 3-4, 5-6. This is sung by the choir as a simple harmonised aria. A dance-like ritornello for instruments interrupts before the second choir sings the same music to the words of the third verse. Once more comes the ritornello; and then three soloists in turn sing the triple-time version of the chant accompanied by a continuo instrument. The emphasis is now strongly on the tune, the hymn almost seeming like the strophic arias which were so popular in the seventeenth-century song books; and in spite of a restatement of the music for the first verse for the ultimate strophe it is this catchy, yet dignified, smooth version which remains in the mind. There were to be several imitations in Venice during the seventeenth century.

This moment of calm, of relative repose puts into high relief the climax of the Vespers which must come in the final *Magnificat*; and it is here that Monteverdi displays all his resources of skill and imagination. There is nothing quite like either of his settings; nor, with due respect to J. S. Bach whose D major setting is as fine as one can reasonably expect, has there ever been since. The text of Mary Magdalene's song is strophic, so it divides naturally into sections. The plainsong must normally be repeated eleven times, a pattern which Monteverdi preserves in essentials, using mainly the 'long note' cantus firmus manner. The natural procedure is seen more clearly in the setting without instruments, though the one using the ensemble naturally differs in detail.

The text is divided into thirteen sections, each using the basic cantus firmus of the *Magnificat*.

Ex.6 *Magnificat*

Ma - gni - fi - cat, anima me - a Do - mi - num—

Each has a distinctive texture and sound, the organ being the constant feature.

Magnificat – tutti
'Anima mea' – for two voices
'Et exultavit' – for three voices
'Quia respexit' – for one voice alone
'Quia fecit' – for six voices in dialogue
'Et misericordia' – for three voices
'Fecit potentiam' – for three voices
'Deposuit' – two sopranos sing in echo
'Esurientes' – for two voices
'Suscepit' – for two voices
'Sicut locutus est' – for five voices in dialogue
'Gloria patri' – for six voices.

The tuttis are in mighty polyphony, the 'Gloria patri' especially so, since the voices chase each other in close canon and, apart from some short episodes in which the plainsong is displayed with organ accompaniment, they are continuously employed. The lighter sections offer greater variety of both sound and emotion. In the trios, one voice usually sings the plainsong while the other two sing an elaborate duet, using florid melody full of bouncing dotted notes and virtuoso scales. The sections for two voices 'paraphrase' the plainsong with the voices singing in honeyed (though never cloying) thirds. The dialogues divide the choir into two groups, which then alternate in the manner of *cori spezzati*. The echo piece repeats the techniques of *Audi, coelum*, except that a third voice makes clear that this is no operatic scena by singing the plainsong (the resulting harmonies are sometimes very strange). The total effect is extraordinary, giving a mixture of the humanity of Mary's song and its universal significance.

If this vocal setting of *Magnificat* is splendid, the one with instruments is still more so. The reason is that the instruments are used idiomatically and therefore open up a complete new range of sound. Monteverdi indeed is not averse to a simple doubling of the voice parts to gain a grander effect: the opening and closing sections have instrumental doublings written into the individual partbooks so that there shall be no mistake (a matter which should, perhaps, make editors and conductors cautious when they do likewise in places where Monteverdi has not so marked). Nor is he incapable of leaving some sections just for voices, as in the 'Et exultavit' with its decorative tenor lines providing counterpoints to the alto's singing of the plainchant; and the 'Et misericorida' which is a simple dialogue between upper and lower groups of the choir, with the plainsong divided almost unnoticed between the upper voices of each. But in the 'Quia respexit' the only vocal line is that of the plainchant sung by the tenors: the instruments play a ritornello suspiciously like a dance, with natty shifting accents; and then accompany the chant with the delicate sounds of flutes and recorders, supported by trombones. It does not sound particularly like church music, though certainly the words 'all generations shall call him blessed' are considerably heightened in meaning by the purity of the wind instruments. The following 'Quia fecit mihi magna' has violins dashing around with great verve; but this is almost conventional compared with 'Deposuit potentes de sede'. This again has only the plainsong for the voice, two violins and two cornetts playing duets above this line. The Mantuan courtiers who heard it first must have instantly recognised the allusion: this is the scene from *L' Orfeo* in which the hero uses the whole power of music to persuade the boatman to ferry him to Hades to find his beloved wife. The cornetts begin with an extraordinarily difficult virtuoso section (using a higher register than that in the opera, which once more has suggested to scholars a transposition down – but perhaps we should use a higher member of the family). The violins come in with a soothing, sweet phrase in thirds, then indulge in some echo effects, to the considerable puzzlement of the organist who has to find chords to fit both, the two being at times in apparant conflict. The echo effects between tenors for the 'Gloria patris' are equally strange at times, though the triumphant declamation of the words by the principal tenor leaves no doubt of the essential meaning of the music, especially since he is kept in the most brilliant part of his voice. And then the 'Sicut erat in principio' provides a victorious dash for home. Mantua has its succession assured, all's right with the world!

Or has it and is it? We know the answer: the house of the Gonzagas was soon to tumble down. As for Monteverdi, the world was never quite right for his depressive nature. But then, his Vespers is not simply grand music for a state occasion. The voluptuousness of the motets, and more than ever the strange stylistic dichotomy of the psalm settings, are both signs of that. When the harmony seems strange in the *Magnificat* echo pieces, the reason is that the plainchant has to remain – it cannot be brushed aside or rewritten as can opera or madrigal. There is a real discipline here, fighting against the modern freedom. This music has certain analogies with the Baroque statuary of the seventeenth century. It is human in its expression of emotion: but the intensity of emotion is almost superhuman. The stillness at the end of *Laudate pueri*, the calm with which *Audi, coelum* concludes, that strange highly perfumed atmosphere in parts of the *Magnificat* – all speak of the mystic, which perhaps Monteverdi was at this time; he was surely at the height of his powers.

We shall never know why he published this music when he did, and in this particular form. In 1610 he was a very unhappy man, recovering still from the nervous breakdown brought about partly by the death of his wife in 1607, partly by the overwork caused by the 1608 opera festival; and no doubt also because of a spiritual crisis which often afflicts those who feel they have arrived at a fame from which there can be only retreat. Anyway, in the year of 1610 he began work on a setting of the Mass, a setting '*di studio e fattica grande*', to quote the words of a friend: words which – however translated – mean firstly that Monteverdi was having to do some conscious thinking about style – his natural manner was not enough – and secondly that he was finding it hard work. The result we now know was the Mass on the motet *In illo tempore* by the Netherlander, Gombert. What was the motive for doing this? There were probably two. One was to include in his volume then in preparation, which was to be dedicated to Pope Paul V, a work which would show that he could make a good *maestro di cappella* for a Roman church, where such tastes were still cultivated. Another was to show that he was no simple revolutionary, but really believed in his theory that there were two 'practices': one in which 'the music [îs] not commanded but commanding, not the servant but the mistress of the words'; the other where expression of the words was paramount. The madrigals and operas showed the latter – as indeed does much of the Vespers music: now he could show them the former – a music of abstract power and perfection of form.

So he chose a motet by a prime practitioner of the 'first practice', the long since dead Gombert, contrapuntist extraordinary; he abstracted themes, several of them closely related to each other; then wrote a Mass on these themes. The scholarly intention is clear since he placed the themes at the top of the first page of the partbooks. Even without this, we would suspect something of the sort because the music is so closely infiltrated with this material. Scarcely a bar goes by without direct use of the themes, deployed with all the contrapuntal devices – inversion, augmentation, diminution – as though it were really and truly an 'Art of fugue'. And although the 'Gombert' Mass is written for a six-part choir, as is Palestrina's *Assumpta est Maria*, almost as to challenge comparison with the great Roman composer, there is none of the sheer glorying in choral sonorities that we find there. Apart from a traditional reduction of forces for the 'Crucifixus', Monteverdi uses the full choir nearly all the time, allowing himself little or no contrast in sound or texture. Certainly he obeys many Palestrinian rules. Dissonance is now an orderly affair of preparation – suspension – resolution and there are none of those maverick discords found in the Vespers music. The melody is deprived of any ornament and is extremely smooth, with neither the expressive leaps so common in his secular music nor the irregular rhythms which make *Lauda Jerusalem* so exciting.

The result, by any rational standards, certainly from the Romantic point of view of the inspiration of works of art, should be academic, which is to say dull: and several writers (including this one) have said so, probably after reading the score rather than listening to the music. In fact, a good performance can convince the listener that there is splendid power in the work. Good performances will indeed be rare. As in the case of certain numbers of the Vespers and indeed the *Assumpta est Maria* Mass, there is a case for transposing the whole piece down to bring it within the more comfortable ranges of the voices. This helps scarcely at all, because this 'Gombert' Mass's continuous deployment of all the voices cannot fail to make it very tiring to sing. Nevertheless, a manuscript copy in Rome, presumably transcribed from a presentation copy to Pope Paul V, shows signs of use, so presumably it was performed there; and a modern recorded performance, taken no doubt with adequate rests in between the actual recording of each section, reveals its glories – which are considerable. The '*studio e fattica*' were undoubtedly worthwhile, and if it would be difficult to assign it to its composer without other evidence, its un-Palestrinian sequences and harmonic drive are enough to show that it is the work of someone still possessed of tremendous energy; and there is something touching about a man who, accused of insidious revolution and wildness, shows a belief in, if not eternal principles, at least historical perspective, order and stability.

Maestro di Cappella at St Mark's

The compositional labours of 1610 did not give the required result, if Monteverdi's intention was to obtain a post in Rome. The publication of that year, on the other hand, was surely to be worthwhile. When the prince whose matrimony Monteverdi had worked so hard to celebrate in 1608 inherited the duchy four years later, one of his first acts was to dismiss a considerable number of artists, including the by now middle-aged composer. Monteverdi naturally felt embittered about this, but there was nothing he could do. After a year of unemployment, he was invited to Venice to see whether he was suitable for the part of director of music at the state church, St Mark's, now unexpectedly vacant on the death of a mediocre but by no means superannuated incumbent. The procurators of St Mark's, cautious as ever, insisted on a *prova*, a public performance of some of his music. We do not know for certain what he chose, but it required a large choir, instrumental ensemble and two chamber organs and was given in the church of S. Giorgio Maggiore on 22 August 1613. What else could it have been but the Vespers – though the documents, it is true, tell of a Mass? Anyway, Monteverdi impressed the officials and was appointed on the spot: he remained in this post for the rest of his life, some thirty years.

It was the first time he had been a church musician, and it must haVe represented a considerable change of life to him. That he composed a great deal of music for St Mark's is certain, for not only was it published in two large retrospective collections, one called *Selva morale* which came out in 1640, the other a posthumous volume of 1650 entitled *Messa et Salmi*, put together perhaps by his pupil Cavalli (frustratingly for us, the nature of these volumes does not allow us to assign dates to pieces written over a considerable number of years); he also published nearly a couple of dozen pieces in various anthologies in the years between 1615 and 1629 (which do allow us to keep track, at least a little, of his developing style). Documents concerning St Mark's and some other Venetian institutions help also in defining the basic conditions under which the music was produced.

In fact, he may have felt more immediately at home in places other than St Mark's, where traditions were rigid and he had new problems to solve. Venice was full of churches and religious confraternities which commissioned music for special holy days. Monteverdi was quickly taken up by one of them. As he wrote delightedly – not without a touch of legitimate malice – to Mantua, where yet another new duke was trying to persuade him to return,

There are useful additional earnings [for a *maestro di cappella*] apart from St Mark's. I have been begged time and again by the Wardens of the Schools [confraternities] and earn 200 ducats a year, for anyone who wants the *maestro di cappella* to make music for them will pay thirty, even forty or as many as fifty ducats for two Vespers and a Mass – and will also thank him very warmly afterwards.

We also know from documents that in at least two years he provided music for the Scuola Grande di S. Rocco. At these institutions, he could not expect the grand forces that he commanded at St Mark's; but he could hire a few excellent singers and no doubt some very capable instrumentalists. Much of the music he contributed to the anthologies is of this kind, and we may assume that, meant for these more modest institutions, these pieces were published because they would be useful elsewhere.

It was natural that he should develop the style of the motets in the Vespers volume, and there are a number of pieces for a single voice as well as duets and trios. Some of them are very fine, especially a group of solo motets published in the mid-1620s. To find a motet asking for Mary's intercession to save the sinner comes as no surprise. *Salve O Regina*, published in 1624, is as passionate as *Nigra sum*, full of virtuosic ornaments for the singer on such vital words as 'Salve', sensual chromaticism for 'gementes et flentes', and wild and sudden outbursts at 'ad te clamamus'. Yet it is well organised with repeated phrases and sections so that it is much more than a piece of religious recitative. It is a true motet; as indeed is a *Salve Regina* published a year later. There are some sobbing trills here, and again chromaticism for 'gementes et flentes', but on the whole the melody is plainer; and woe betide the singer who adds vulgar ornaments instead of allowing the beauty of his *messa di voce* to make the expressive points. Most of all there is a harmonic command, reminiscent of *Pulchra es* in the Vespers, which takes the attention away from pure *bel canto* and underlines the words 'Et Jesum benedictum fructum ventris tui . . .' Not that Monteverdi has fought the eroticism of the *Song of Songs*. *O quam pulchra es* turns up in this same anthology set as lusciously as ever, with *trilli* and long roulades, falling sixths, and some sultry chromaticisms for 'Veni quia amore langueo'. But here we notice that there are considerable passages in triple time which can only be called 'tuneful', with balanced phrases and memorable fragments of melody. This is a trait common to much Venetian music in the 1620s and Monteverdi puts it to good use in other motets, especially those with cheerful texts: for one result of setting texts in praise of saints on festival days is that cheerfulness keeps breaking in – a new experience for a man so bowed down by fate in his later Mantuan years. One deliciously happy piece is *Currite populi*, a motet in praise of any saint you care for (the name is left blank in the original). Its opening section is an arietta which would have pleased any publisher, as a potential hit (Ex. 7 overleaf).

Exulta filia takes this attitude a shade further. It also begins with a joyful triple-time tune, which is encased in an equally happy ritornello to be played (and largely invented from the bass line) by the continuo player. But the piece is built on a large scale, Monteverdi splitting it up into several well-defined sections, one of arioso-recitative, another

Ex.7   *Currite populi*

[note values reduced]

a brilliant, virtuosic 'alleluia', so that it becomes virtually a miniature cantata. Best of all these solo motets, however, is *Laudate Dominum*, in which Monteverdi shows a flair for writing catchy melody; for showing off the cleverness of the singer (there is some difficult ornamentation as well as the necessity for breath control in long phrases); for organisation (much of the piece is built on the same chaconne bass figure which he used in his well-known secular duet *Zefiro torna*); as well as for painting the words vividly, as the fanfares for the psalmist's demand to 'praise him with the trumpet' show (Ex. 8).

There is little difference between these works and Monteverdi's secular music, except perhaps that they tend to be slightly less extravagant in dissonance, smoother in melody and slightly more closely organised in pattern. This is underlined by three solo motets which do seem more operatic (as indeed one is), being an arrangement

Ex.8 *Laudate Dominum*

of the famous *Lamento d' Arianna* as the *Pianto della Madonna*, (set to Latin words, in spite of the Italian title). The *Lament* had, of course, become the first operatic scena to be published as a separate number and was one of the most famous pieces of the era, so that a total removal from its operatic context was normal by the time it was printed in the *Selva morale*. It works surprisingly well in its new guise and was surely the model for some of Carissimi's similar pieces in such an oratorio as *Jepthe*. The other two 'operatic' motets are for bass, and exploit the large range from baritone register to true bass notes in such a way that one could almost swear they were written for that singer who took the part of Charon in *L' Orfeo* (1607) and Pluto in the *Ballo delle Ingrate* (1608). *Laudate Dominum* is relatively straight-forward, with some roulades giving way to smoother, aria-like triple time: the roulades return for the 'Amen', the final phrase moving swiftly from top to bottom of the voice in the same manner as that in which Purcell exploited the voice of his famous John Gostling. More remarkable still is *Ab aeterno ordinata sum*, with words suggesting a

Hades scene – another link with the early operas. Here are vast leaps from top notes to bottom. There is even a low C for 'abissos' – and no amount of transposition will help, considering the top Ds immediately before. The word painting is extravagant with rolling semiquavers for 'girovallabant'; but there is flowing melody for 'et delitiae meae esse cum filiis hominum'. This piece is like a detail from a 'Last Judgement' of some Baroque painter: vivid, lifelike, yet still religious in aim and attitude.

The surviving duets are fewer and on the whole less impressive – surprisingly since, in secular music, this was a genre into which Monteverdi poured some of his finest ideas. Not that they lack pleasant music. *Cantate Domino* has a tuneful refrain made more honeyed by the sweet thirds between the sopranos: still more tuneful is *O beatae viae*, composed for the Scuola di S. Rocco, probably in the year of its publication, 1620. And *Fugge, anima mea*, perhaps destined for another musical confraternity, the Scuola di S. Giovanni Evangelista, is both melodious and capable of some neat word painting. But the only pieces which really challenge the solo motets in intensity are two settings of *Salve Regina*. One, indeed, really is a solo, for the second voice is only an echo: but Monteverdi introduces two violins in the middle of the piece to harmonise the smooth melody of intercession, 'O Maria, Virgo, O Mater misericordiae', so that it seems concertante rather than monodic. It is in atmosphere very like the echo section in the 1610 *Magnificat*, the echo voice suggesting the same sort of harmonies – and in the final section the solo tenor and violins indulge in some almost erotic chromaticism. Finer still, in my view, is a setting for two tenors in which there are no restrictions caused by echo effects. The words here are made almost painfully into a plea for personal grace, and the final cry for help is Bernini-esque in its anguish (Ex. 9).

The setting of the same text for three voices which immediately follows in the *Selve morale* could not be finer: but it is not less so. Monteverdi has the possibility of real counterpoint to add to the monodic effects. In the solo sections, the harmony often has those astringent irregularities which infect his madrigals and early operas. In the trio sections, a chromatic line imitated through all the voices produces an equal intensity, and again the final bars, in which the upper voices rise chromatically, with imitations pushing the voices forward over a held pedal note in the bass, are superbly emotional (Ex. 10 overleaf).

Ex.9 *Salve Regina*

If, as I have suggested, many of these works were written for small organisations (musically speaking), some may undoubtedly have been performed also in St Mark's. But as *maestro di cappella* of the basilica, Monteverdi's role was somewhat different. Though the details of the musical requirements of the church for this time have not been found, there are sufficient documents from a later era to make it clear that he inherited a precise schedule. There were grand festivals when Mass or Vespers (or both) were given splendid music. For some of them, there had to be psalms or *Magnificat* for double choir. On these days he could count on not only a choir of almost twenty-five singers, but a similarly sized orchestra if he liked (his stable number of players was sixteen[1] after 1614 and he could add extras as required). His choir was supposed to sing Mass every day,

[1] Archivio di Stato, Venice, Proc. de Supra, Registro 141 f9v.

Ex.10 *Salve Regina*

[Basso continuo doubles the bass line]

and there was probably a roster so that they need not all attend each weekday, just as the two organists of the basilica tended to alternate. Monteverdi was under no obligation to direct every day, though there was pressure on him to do so on festivals.

Discipline had become slack as far as the ordinary days were concerned. Monteverdi, the new broom, revived the custom of sung (daily) Masses, buying in works by the Romans – Palestrina among them – from the local Venetian presses. He also added to the repertoire himself, though only two Masses by him in this style survive. His year of '*studio e fattica*' came in handy. It is clear that he was now fluent in the old style, and these two Masses flow more naturally than had the 'Gombert' paraphrase. Since these were for ordinary days, they were written for a four-voiced choir accompanied by organ and did not demand the strenuous efforts of the earlier work. There are indeed ample rests, as Monteverdi reverted to the earlier Netherlandish practice of contrasting the upper and lower two sections of the choir. Nor are these pieces consciously learned. There is no parading of themes at the head of the Kyrie; and although he worked out his material quite thoroughly, he was willing to break off strict contrapuntal writing to make an expressive point, as in the G minor Mass at the words 'et iterum venturus est'.

Ex.11 *Messa a 4 v.*

[note values reduced]

Although it is difficult to pinpoint it exactly, one gains the impression that Monteverdi now found it easier to manipulate the harmonic and melodic restrictions in a way which came more naturally to the seventeenth-century composer. Passing notes can produce unusual chords, and discords on the stressed beats are not always strictly 'prepared' in the previous chord. There is a distinct sense of modern tonality: this music does not sound particularly 'antique' because the old modal system has gone. The rhythms are also more modern because they are more regular, and there are occasional extended melismas which look as though they could have been written by Palestrina but in practice seem almost like — admittedly rather conservative – ornaments. And if the F major Mass (printed in the *Selva morale*) is rather dry in its refusal to exploit choral sonorities, the G minor has some moments of distinctive brilliance. As with the 'Gombert' Mass, there is a case for making a substantial transposition downward, singing the top line with counter-tenors. Either way, the 'qui tollis peccata mundi' will sound glorious, and the following 'miserere nobis' will bring the work quietly, almost intimately to an end. In fact, though one might believe that works in such a studied style must be cold, Monteverdi's changing personality is reflected quite well in his three *stile antico* Masses. If in Mantua he was tense, determined to show the world his skill and passion, in Venice he was more relaxed, more philosophical in accepting (as the Most Serene Republic itself was doing) increasing age. There is almost a sense of relief and calm in the works.

His interest in the *stile antico* was not confined to settings of the Mass. There were several psalm settings pervaded by the old manner, though not completely dominated by it. Monteverdi says as much in one setting of *Laudate pueri* which is marked 'a 5 [voci] da capella'. It looks less obviously to be in the old manner, since the 'white notes' of the Masses are replaced by the 'black notes', or halved-note values of modern music. A more detailed examination reveals that it is only this superficial feature which is different. Here are the same contrapuntal textures, indeed many of the same turns of phrase as in the 'Gombert' Mass, complete with those rolling sequences which were such a hallmark of that work; and there is that Monteverdian quip of returning to the opening music at the words 'sicut erat in principio'. The themes are similarly regular in rhythm and the harmony equally follows the Palestrinian principles, albeit occasionally with a modest freedom. But the exploitation of sonority is here much more enterprising, and if the wording in the *basso continuo* part 'alla quarta bassa' implies the customary transposition, with the falsettists of St Mark's on the upper parts, the ascending phrase for 'et super Caelos gloria eius' can hardly have failed to thrill the listeners. There is also a setting of *Lauda Jerusalem* for five voices in the same style, though here memories of the 1610 Vespers are stronger since the soprano part opens with the plainsong cantus firmus in long notes, though it gives it up when it is needed to add weight to the imitative counterpoint (it returns, predictably, with the 'sicut erat'). There is a great deal of word painting, chromaticism for 'et liquefaciet ea', flowing melismas for 'et fluent aquae'. The general effect is therefore less that of a *stile antico* piece than of a madrigal in the sixteenth-century manner, though the themes are squarer, the matching accentuation of words and music less subtle. It is nonetheless a fine work.

To find the *stile antico* creeping into the pieces for double choir is more surprising, for the psalms of the Vespers had been distinctly modern in attitudes. Yet by the time Monteverdi arrived in Venice, the ways of *cori spezzati* were becoming distinctly old-fashioned. It is interesting that the later motets of the best-known representative of the old Venetian school, Giovanni Gabrieli, rarely are simply polychoral, although the old format may be retained. But the contrasting forces will be a ripieno choir, soloists accompanied by organ, a large instrumental ensemble, pitted against each other on strictly unequal terms, each being written idiomatically so that the motets become sectional – cantata-like – as indeed had Monteverdi's settings of the *Magnificat* in the 1610 volume. The true polychoral manner with, literally, two or more choirs of voices (perhaps supported, but not dominated, by instruments and instrumental style) continued mainly in the Venetian provinces on the mainland, in Rome, and especially in Germany, where it became extremely popular. However, the Gabrielian modifications took over even in Germany, leading to that orgy of polychoralism – the so-called *Missa Salzburgensis* – probably written for some great occasion in Salzburg Cathedral, for which the town musicians, the trumpets and drums of the local military, the consorts of viols and violins, every choirboy and male singer, were pressed into service.

Monteverdi's music for double choir is not in this manner. His Venetian masters apparently demanded the Vespers music to be sung thus on occasion, for virtually all his double-choir music consists either of settings of psalms or of the *Magnificat*. Two of the former might almost have been written a century earlier. *Credidi* indeed looks as though Monteverdi had been studying the first published psalms *a cori spezzati*, those of Willaert (a contemporary of Gombert), deploying two modest choirs of voices (no necessity for instruments here) and an organist who does no more than double the lowest bass part. The Willaertian rule that each choir must make harmonic sense independently (a sensible attitude, if the listener is nearer one choir than the other) is obeyed. The harmony is strongly consonant, the rhythms staid, with only a little very temporary excitement at the 'Gloria patri'. There is some quasi-Gabrielian dialogue, the choirs vying with each other in quiet succession, but the mood is dignified rather than dynamic. Much the same can be said of *Memento*, though the rhythms are a shade more lively and there are one or two direct passages and some points of imitation, rather than the solid chordal blocks of *Credidi*. The words 'inimicos ejus' suggest a warlike exchange between the choirs and 'efflorebit sanctificatio mea' some figuration. But otherwise this is Venice becoming ossified, solemn, 'most serene' in fact, rather than passionate.

The double-choir works where Monteverdi takes up the techniques developed in the *Laudate pueri Dominum* of the 1610 volume are more lively. The essence of those techniques was the acknowledgement that the existence of an accompanying organ playing from a *basso continuo* allows the contrasts to be not simply between the two choirs, but between tutti and soloists, between solid choral sound and duets and trios. One of the first works of this kind is the first setting of *Dixit Dominus* printed in the 1650 volume. It begins with some solemn chords from both choirs which look as though the conservatism of *Memento* and *Credidi* is to win here also; but come the words 'sede a dextris' there arrives a duet from the two altos of the two choirs – or rather a trio, for the soprano of Choir I now starts singing a 'long note' cantus firmus. Shades of the Vespers! Though the comparison will not quite suffice. This *Dixit* is both less intellectually conceived and less passionately felt. The use of the cantus firmus technique is only intermittently applied; while the duets and trios seem, after the Mantuan Vespers, almost austere, what few ornaments there are being rather restrained and most of the melody being rather plain. Nor are there any extravagant dissonances or violent contrasts. Nonetheless the music is fine, with dynamic blows for tutti on the words 'confregit in die irae suae reges'; an outburst of splendid grandeur for 'implebit ruinas' and a honeyed duet for alto and tenor of the first choir for 'De torrente'; finishing with a warm rather than brilliant 'Amen' which is very satisfying.

In the same vein is a setting of the *Magnificat* 'a 8 voci et due violini et quattro viole overo quattro Tromboni quali in acidente si ponno lasciare',[1] the very designation for performance reminding us of the Venetian penchant for brass instruments. It has a very old-fashioned time signature and its opening bars, written in white notes rather than the more modern 'black' ones, might give the impression that the double choir has again suggested the *stile antico*. But then the time signature indicates a triple measure, and it is soon evident that this is an almost dance-like measure, as it progresses to the words 'et exultavit spiritus meus'. By this time it is also clear that the double-choir format is something of an irrelevance: there is no dialogue

[1] 'for 8 voices and 2 violins and 4 viols or 4 trombones which can be omitted in case of need.'

between the choirs, and although no doubt they were stationed in the separated galleries in St Mark's, the real contrasts are between various groups of solo voices and the tutti (for the two choirs are invariably used together). The tutti is used imaginatively. There is some impressive sonority for 'fecit mihi magna'; chromaticism for 'Et misericordia'; splendidly pugilistic fanfares in that warlike style, the *stile concitato* which Monteverdi was developing in the 1620s, for 'fecit potentiam in brachio'. Nevertheless, the main interest is given to the soloists, who are capable of mellifluous duets in triple time (the sweet thirds for 'humilitatem ancillae suae' are especially appealing) as well as one formidable roulade for 'dispersit' in which one can imagine that much sought-after castrato sound ('hoch und hell' – high and bright – as Lasso once called it) making a splendid effect. And we are reminded of the Vespers grand *Magnificat* when first one tenor, then the other, lets out a great cry of 'Gloria' at the beginning of the doxology.

Ex.12 *Magnificat: 'Gloria'*

But it is significant that this *Magnificat* differs from that of the 1610 collection firstly by being totally 'unoperatic' (Venice had not as yet been infected with that particular taste) and secondly by being in truth unsectional. One can divide this piece into sections, but the music seems to flow on throughout, since there is no feeling that this or that section is (more or less) complete in itself because of a different sound or texture. Monteverdi has accepted the idea of a different kind of church music, one stemming from the now universal concertato motet of the Viadana school.

This tradition is at the root of most of his other church music for St Mark's, though it varies from pieces which are very nearly church music of a kind which hardly needs a *basso continuo* part to those in which the pattern of the continuo line governs the whole shape of the piece. The former is true of four masterly motets which were published in 1620 in a volume of music by an erstwhile Mantuan colleague, Giulio Cesare Bianchi – and which must have done much to ensure its sales. The first of them, *Cantate Domino*, might be called a 'choral madrigal' (remembering that most madrigals were sung by consorts of soloists) for the motifs and certain turns of phrase are certainly madrigalian. One section is based on an idea first used in the famous *Ecco mormorar l'onde* from his *Second Book of Madrigals*, published thirty years earlier:

Ex.13   *Cantate Domino*

This time the texture is kept full for much of the time, to make a more resonant sound than is found in the madrigal. The same is true of a setting of *Domine, ne in furore tuo*, a penitential psalm which has some splendidly sonorous homophony, and uses the deeper male voices of St Mark's choir most effectively.

The two most emotional of these motets, however, reserve the sonority of the tutti for climaxes and lighten the texture by using the organ to accompany the smaller groups of voices. *Christe, adoramus te* is a declamatory, passionate piece, depicting the agony on the Cross by chromatic melody, and giving the plea for redemption increased personal significance by the use of a solo voice supported by the organ. This piece was probably written about 1618 for the Festival of the Holy Cross, for a piece of the True Cross was one of some newly discovered relics in the Treasury of St Mark's. *Adoramus te* may have been written for the same occasion, since the piece of the Cross was stained (so it was said) with the Blood of Our Saviour. It would be just possible to sing this motet without the organ – though not very satisfactory in some places – since this too is a choral madrigal and has a beautiful short section reminiscent of the madrigals in his *Third Book* (1592) written for an ensemble including three women's voices. But here the uppermost line would not tax the resources of a good counter-tenor and, indeed, the concluding prayer 'miserere mundi' again is scored to reap the maximum sounds from the lower voices. There is none of the sensuous ecstatic chromaticism of *Christe adoramus te*; rather does it rely on gentler but unexpected shifts of harmony and some delicate counterpoint. It is an economical yet strong piece by a master of both choral sound and madrigalian intensity.

Economy of both resource and resources indeed is everywhere to be found in Monteverdi's music for St Mark's. It is enough to have a single voice and a small ensemble of stringed instruments for beautiful, melodious yet varied music to appear. The *Selva morale* includes a group of hymns for one, two or three voices – most are written in the soprano clef but could just as easily be sung an octave lower by tenors – with two violins and *basso continuo* which would suit a small church or confraternity, as well as any basilica or princely church. Moreover, they are suitable for almost any saint's day since, as Monteverdi writes at the head of the first setting of *Sanctorum meritis*, 'you may sing the same tune [*aria*] to any other hymns that are in the same metre'.[1] The word '*aria*' is appropriate: these hymns are really very like the arias of the contemporary song books. This setting of *Sanctorum meritis* is a hemiola song like *Ave maris stella*, with an engaging little ritornello which would not have been too much out of place among the composer's *Scherzi musicali* of 1607. The setting of *Iste confessor* which is also printed with the words of *Ut queant laxis* for the Festival of St John the Baptist is just as tuneful. It opens with a short, slightly solemn overture. Then comes a catchy ritornello, finishing with a little sweet dialogue between the violins. Finally, the 'aria' arrives, sung by a soprano: and the tune is certainly memorable (Ex. 14 overleaf). The closing bars echo the final bars of the ritornello (hence the violin dialogue, to make the motif stick in the mind): the ritornello returns and a second verse is sung by the other sopranos (when in St Mark's from the other choir gallery?). After the repeat of the ritornello, both sopranos sing the tune in

---

[1] It is worth noting that Monteverdi sets only every other verse of each hymn and those omitted should be sung to plainsong.

Ex.14   *Iste Confessor*

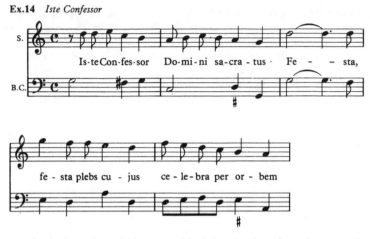

thirds, before the whole ensemble joins in the 'Amen', to music reminiscent of the overture.

But perhaps the most pleasing of all the hymns is the setting of *Deus tuorum militum* for alto (or tenor), tenor and bass, with two violins and continuo. No overture or ritornello here to delay the entry of the alto voice, which announces the first phrase of the melody in smooth triple time. The violins echo the voice, the bass sings the second phrase and is similarly answered by the instruments (its phrase actually persists in the *basso continuo* line and therefore may not be noticed). The tenor proceeds to the third phrase – but instead of a balancing phrase from the violins, the voices join together in a brief madrigalian section *à 3*. As often with Monteverdi, there is a tinge of melancholy as an expected major harmony is twisted into a chord with a flattened seventh:

Ex.15   *Deus tuorum militum*

A ritornello eventually arrives to give a gap between verses: and there is the usual solemn 'Amen'. 'This aria can be used for *Jesu corona virginum, Christe Redemptor omnium* and other hymns of the same metre': indeed – and why not, since one could hear it every day without tiring of the music's smoothness and slight pinpricks of harmony?

A solo voice or two seems a natural for hymns: it is more surprising to find a similar ensemble of voices and strings employed in setting a psalm, since psalms are usually long and cry out for greater contrasts. In fact, Monteverdi set *Confitebor tibi* (Psalm 110) for a solo soprano and violins twice; and once again for just soprano and tenor with violins. Why he chose this psalm to set so modestly is difficult to say; but all three settings are interesting and do not outstay their welcome. In one sense, the version easiest to explain is that printed in the *Selva morale* with the rubric *'alla francese a 5 voci* which may also be performed [*concertare*] if you like with *quattro viole da brazzo* [i.e. members of the violin family] leaving the soprano part to be sung by a solo voice'. The term *alla francese* – in the French style – has been the subject of much scholarly discussion and we are still not quite sure of its meaning. The most likely explanation is that Monteverdi was imitating some of the chansons written around 1600 in the so-called *musique mesurée*, in which there was an attempt to imitate the rhythms used by the ancient Greeks, as interpreted by various French thinkers on music. Thus the syllables were divided into long and short, which were generally then given notes in the ratio of length 1 : 2 (the detailed discussions were much more sophisticated than this, but this explanation will serve present purposes). Thus phrases tend to be very orderly in rhythm, in contrast to that fluidity with which Italians set their native tongue in the attempt to follow a natural speech rhythm. The other trait of this 'French style' is that phrases are often sung first by a soloist, then repeated harmonised by a five-part choir. Monteverdi wrote two madrigals in this style, one well known today, *Dolcissimo uscignolo*, the other less so, *Chi vol haver felice*. He published both in 1638 in his eighth book of madrigals, the *Madrigals of War and Love*, a collection including music going back to at least 1608; so it may well be that these pieces date from the early years of the century. He reworks material from both in this setting of *Confitebor*, though a touch of warlike *stile concitato* at the word 'terribile' indicates that this was written rather later. Still, the French manner is certainly there. The rhythms and phrase lengths are orderly: many are repeated by a choir – or, as Monteverdi indicates, a group of strings. The tunefulness of the piece is self-evident, and if one might feel that it is a shade too charming and lacking in power, the doxology settles the issue with one of those gorgeous virtuosic cries of 'Gloria patri' which seem to be almost a hallmark of the composer from the 1610 settings of the *Magnificat* onward; to which is eventually added an appropriate *da capo* for 'Sicut erat in principio' and a dignified 'Amen' very like those in the hymns.

The other *Confitebor* for a single voice, marked '*a voce sola con violini*' in the 1650 volume, also has a touch of Frenchness in its regularity, rhythms tending to be repeated to form rounded phrases; and there are one or two turns of melody just near enough to *alla francese* setting to make one suspect that this was an attempt at something similar. It begins with a brief but solemn overture, which might well open a *balletto alla francese*. This develops into a rather jolly ritornello which keeps returning throughout the piece. Soon it is evident that this is a show piece for a great castrato and there is some naughtiness in the way that Monteverdi toys with the words 'fidelia' (Exx. 16a and 16b) and 'sanctum'. But there is sensuousness in the chromatic phrases setting 'initium sapientiae timor Domini'; and an echo 'Amen', the first violin taking the part of the distant voice, which again reminds us of the Mantuan Vespers music.

Monteverdi's *Confitebor a due voci con due Violini* develops the same idea. The overture: the ritornello (more plainly derived from the dance, since it is in triple time with hemiolas); the melodious phrases which are now plentiful ('fidelia' is now divided between the voices in an otherwise almost identical phrase); chromaticism for 'initium sapientiae timor Domini' – all these are very similar, though the fierceness of the setting of 'et terribile nomen eius' is more powerful. If the 'Gloria' is set more mellifluously, Monteverdi makes up in strength with an 'Amen', more elaborate than in the other version, echo following echo as though he could not bear to leave it.

Such pieces might have been written for any of those confraternities where the *Guardian Grande* was willing to offer Monteverdi fifty ducats for two Vespers and a Mass – and 'thank him very warmly afterwards'. But in the larger-scale pieces which surely must have been written for festivals at St Mark's it is evident that Monteverdi had a penchant for putting the solo voice to good use. It was probably a matter of making a virtue out of necessity. The choir doubtless had its excellent singers; but since nobody was ever

Ex.16 *Confitebor*

(a)

fi - de - - li - a   fi - de - - li - a - - a -

(b)

- a   fi - de - li - a   San - - -

tr

- - - - - ctum.

pensioned off, and even the most ancient were expected to perform their duties on the great days of State, the full choir cannot always have been very good. The problem had been evident to some of Monteverdi's predecessors and both Giovanni Croce, *maestro di cappella* from 1603 to 1609, and Giovanni Gabrieli, organist until the year before Monteverdi's arrival, had sought ways of differentiating between the skilled and less skilled. They had experimented mainly with the motet, composing psalms and masses either contrapuntally or for double choir. For Monteverdi the motet, where one could choose one's text, was – as we have seen – better composed either in a madrigalian way or for a small group of favoured voices. Vesper psalms were the real problem. Lengthy texts which could not be altered required some method of organisation to make them musically coherent: these were what the *maestro di cappella* had to provide for many large festivals, and they fill the greater part of both retrospective volumes of his church music.

If there were violins, the problems could be resolved by using ritornellos here and there. Why not do something similar with the ripieno singers? The answer should have been that singers sing words, and to repeat words at different stages of the psalm is to make nonsense of the text; or if the same music is given to different words, surely there will be a discrepancy between the meaning of the two. Neither objection seemed strange to a composer who, after all, had written an opera in which the 'tedium of the recitative' (to quote, admittedly, a later writer) was never allowed to get in the way of musical shaping: which is why *L'Orfeo* is a masterpiece and the *Euridice* operas of the Florentines Peri and Caccini are not.

So when Monteverdi sets out to write a *Lauda Jerusalem* for just three voices – alto, tenor and bass – he makes some delicate adjustments in the text. No chance of the glorious sound of the Mantuan setting – in Venice he surely had less rehearsal as well as less virtuoso forces. So he opens with a vigorous triple-time section for all three voices, working out a short contrapuntal tag which seems to express the sheer joy of the psalmist. Solemn chords (marked 'tutti' in the organ part) follow in duple time from the words 'Quoniam confortavit seras portarum tuarum'. The dancing triples return and there is a huge section in which there is some nice word painting: dynamic rhythms for 'velociter currit sermo eius', virtuoso melismas for 'spargit', before a cadence is arrived at. At 'mittit Crystalum suum' the tutti music heard at 'Quoniam' returns. There is another trio with word painting, smooth chromatic melody being inspired by 'liquefaciet' and scales for 'fluent aquae'. Then comes the doxology and the tutti music returns. All seems over when, at 'sicut erat in principio et semper', Monteverdi decides to repeat the final word 'semper . . . semper, lauda lauda': the psalmist's praises return to Monteverdi's opening music. Only then is the psalm allowed to proceed to its close and, as we might expect, to the tutti music, to which is added an 'Amen'. This is a lithe rather than an emotional setting, full of energy and solemnity, and showing a slightly cooler atmosphere than Monteverdi's earlier style had conveyed.

The same technique and much the same emotional quality is found in the first setting of *Confitebor tibi* printed in the *Selva morale* with the rubric 'for three voices with five other voices as ripieno'. Again trio sections are punctuated by chordal tuttis (this time the full choir including the sopranos), these using the identical music for first 'Magna opera Domini', 'Ut det illis', 'Sanctum et terribile' and the 'Gloria Patri' and 'semper et in saecula' in the doxology. In a setting of *Laudate pueri*[1] which was never published but was apparently taken back to Germany in 1628 by Schütz after his second stay in Venice, the sonorous refrain retains its first words 'Laudate pueri Dominum, laudate nomen Domini'. The variety comes in the solo sections in between, some duets for tenors, quartets for other combinations of voices and a set of short phrases for individual singers which end with a virtuoso solo for bass, perhaps for the same man for which *Ab aeterno* was written. The symmetry of this setting makes it seem classical rather than passionate: it is serious, even solemn, always interesting but never extravagant.

If such methods had a Venetian tradition behind them, Monteverdi also liked the forms controlled by bass patterns that he had used in the Mantuan Vespers. The use of an ostinato bass became especially fashionable in the 1620s, Banchieri writing a whole mass on the 'aria del Granduca' – a pattern lasting seventeen bars occurring throughout, with little relief from other material. Tarquinio Merula, organist and master of the choristers at Bergamo Cathedral, did the same in 1640, rather proudly pointing out the fact in his preface that his work was 'made upon a cantus fermus' (shades of the Vespers!) and one commentator says that the 'work is on a bass of few beats repeated hundreds of times'.[2] Monteverdi's most extreme addiction to the genre is a setting of *Laetatus sum* 'for two violins and two voices, two basses or bassoons' as one of the partbooks says, not too accurately: for if it makes the point that the instruments and voices are in pairs, in fact there are pairs of sopranos, tenors, basses, trombones and violins in addition to the solitary bassoon. In the *basso continuo* book there is printed a series of just four notes:

Ex.17 *Laetatus sum*

To this is appended a note telling the player to keep on playing it until the words 'propter Fratres' occur – a matter of repeating the

[1] Kassel, Murhardsche und Landesbibliothek music manuscript fol. 51 v (new edition, Oxford University Press, 1982).

[2] G. Gaspari, *Catalogo della Biblioteca Musicale G. B. Martini di Bologna* (Bologna, 1890, reprinted 1961) II p. 271.

pattern one hundred and six times; whereupon the pattern changes to triple time and is repeated yet thirty-five more times. Come the doxology, and the pattern is briefly broken, though its resumption for 'semper' seems inevitable and there are some fifteen repetitions to bring the psalm to an end. Over this constant and very restrictive bass, the pairing of forces leads to a set of duets – for violins, for sopranos, for tenors punctuated by trombones, and for basses with surprisingly virtuosic interjections by bassoon (there is ample evidence from elsewhere that there was an excellent player called Giovanni Sansoni[1] in St Mark's). It sounds a perfect recipe for utter boredom: in the event it proves very exciting. The tension is kept up by the feeling that surely soon the dam must burst, the ostinato figure must be abandoned. But the duets are varied enough to keep the piece in motion until the abolition of the structure. There are witty short phrases for the violins; smoothly flowing ones for the upper voices; the basses, on the other hand, take to brilliant semiquavers. In the triple time, the voices gradually come together to give an increasing sense of climax which finally arrives in the solemn chords of 'Gloria patri et filio'.

The same method is deployed more moderately in probably the most famous piece of all Monteverdi's Venetian church music, the *Beatus primo à 6 voci concertato con due violini et 3 viole da brazzo ovvero 3 Tromboni quali anco si ponno lasciare*, which, being translated, means that one must have at least six voices and two violins to which may be added three lower members of the violin family (perhaps violas and cellos) or three trombones with a continuo instrument (surely the organ). The optional parts were not printed, but can be constructed without too much difficulty from the lower voice parts. The bass pattern here is longer.

Ex.18 *Beatus vir*

[1] One of the younger composers associated with St Mark's, Dario Costello, wrote some instrumental works with elaborate bassoon parts in the 1620s. See E. Selfridge-Field, *Venetian Instrumental Music from Gabrieli to Vivaldi* (Oxford, 1975).

Better still, it can be varied without too much bother, the first bars being repeated once, twice or three times at will, while the remainder can be changed in minor details. The texture is now not confined merely to a series of duets, but is quite unpredictable, varying from solo phrases to those for the whole ensemble. Interestingly, the violins sometimes play music which the voices would be hard put to sing – something which Monteverdi has transplanted from the source of the main themes of the piece, his catchy duet *Chiome d'oro*, published in 1619 with words of the kind which the late Thurston Dart aptly characterised as 'amorous baby-talk'. The result is more human than the *Laetatus sum*, though the overall pattern is not much different, even to the lengthy central section in triple time. There is the opportunity to do a little word painting: militaristic semiquavers for 'irascetur', a dashing, suddenly broken-off fragment for 'fremet' and a dying fall for 'peribit'. Monteverdi does not hesitate to bring back his opening theme, with hints of the favoured Venetian rondo when he wants a climax. The result is tuneful, on the whole happy, and yet sonorous enough for a state festival.

Another setting for seven voices with violins, printed in 1650, is less famous but scarcely less attractive – and perhaps a shade more profound. This is a subtle rondo, even though at times it seems to have echoes of an ostinato. The descending bass in the opening bars seems as though it might be shaping for a romanesca or other stock pattern: the tune for the sopranos is not particularly striking, indeed perhaps rather a casual phrase in the major. The words 'Blessed is he that fearest the Lord' are extended into the next section, a trio punctuated by a short violin ritornello. The full ensemble comes in for the words 'potens in terra' (mighty on earth shall be his seed, 'earth' equally suggesting a downward leap). Then, just as we are expecting the psalm to proceed on its concertante way, the opening is brought back unchanged, but obviously gathering significance. 'Glory and wealth shall be in his house' sing all the voices in turn, but before the section has time to finish the sopranos burst in with the opening, superimposing it over the other parts. A tenor solo impassionedly tells us that for the righteous man there is light among the darkness: before it is finished the violins come in with the 'Beatus' theme, leading to the entry of the sopranos – now in the minor and equally passionate. So the opening keeps coming back, differing in context and harmony, sometimes obviously emotional, sometimes (as when the rest of the choir hold deeply-scored chords) rather grandly: and so it is to the end. This is less stately than its famous brother, yet one cannot help finding Monteverdi making it a cry of hope. 'The desire of the wicked shall perish', ends the psalmist, but Monteverdi finishes with 'Blessed is the man that feareth the Lord'.

We have no way of dating these works, but one piece can be assigned to a particular occasion, and it is so similar to these settings of *Beatus vir* that we will not be far wrong in considering them to belong to the same epoch. The work is a *Gloria à 7 voci* printed in the *Selva morale*. In 1630 a great plague came to Venice, in spite of stringent precautions, and killed a huge number – forty thousand or more – of the population. The life of the city virtually ceased for over a year and when the infection had died down, the state authorities decided to build a votive church, S. Maria della Salute, and to hold a Mass of thanksgiving in St Mark's. This service took place on 20 November 1631 and a booklet describing it tells us that 'there was sung the most solemn mass, composed by the *maestro di cappella*, Claudio Monteverdi, the glory of our century. In the Gloria and Credo, trombones were added to the voices, giving an exquisite and wonderful music.' In the *Selva morale* there are two alternative sections to the Credo in the modern style which may, it is said, take the place of those in the *stile antico* in the Mass for four voices already described (see p. 41). There has been some discussion as to whether that means that the Mass for this day of thanksgiving consisted of the Kyrie, Sanctus and Agnus Dei of the Mass for four voices, together with the Credo given with three interpolations and the large-scale Gloria which is next to them in the volume; or whether really only the Gloria survives in full and the interpolations to the Credo are part of a grander conception, a true *Missa concertata*, of which most of the music has disappeared. Either is a possible view. By 1630 Masses were not considered the musical units which had been normal fifty years earlier (there is a fine mass by Monteverdi's assistant Alessandro Grandi, which mixes up styles in a surprising but not unacceptable way and was published in this very year), and we should not assume that a performance of the *stile antico* movements with the 'modern' section is inconceivable. Be this as it may, there is no doubt about one thing: the *Gloria a 7* is a superb setting which can well stand by itself.

It is a very Venetian piece, scored for virtually double choir (though the partbooks don't make this clear), which, however, is treated in the concertante way of the great settings of the *Magnificat* rather than as a source of dialogue, with two independent violin parts and optional (though very desirable) parts for trombones or strings which the conductor or editor must deduce from the voice parts. The design is on an ample scale. The opening is splendid, relishing choral sound and coming to a good climax. But at the words 'et in terra pax' there is stillness, slow chords rich with passing notes being carefully scored to use the lowest registers of each part. With the return to praise at 'Laudamus te' an extended series of bright duets for violins, sopranos and tenors is very reminiscent of the famous *Beatus vir*. This is interrupted at the 'Gratias' where the word 'Gloriam' suggests a return to the opening music (the Venetian rondo is still with us). Then comes one of the most remarkable and beautiful passages: a brief soprano duet, 'Domine Deus', is thrice interrupted by a fierce choral section with strong rhythms; and then leads into what is in effect a huge strophic variation with three verses, one for sopranos with bass voice, one for tenors and one for basses, each over the same harmonic progressions, each punctuated by a sweet ritornello for violins. There is more concertante interplay between the various groups of voices. At the words 'Tu solus altissimus Jesu Christe' there are solemn effective chords, and then at the 'in gloria Dei patri, Amen', the opening music comes back yet once more to bring the work to a rousing conclusion.

From this piece it is not difficult to see why the commentator called Monteverdi 'the glory of our century'. It is remarkably fine, not only in its public face – the sonority traditional to Venice – but in its tender moments, such as the soprano duets, and its moments of calm and mystery, as in the 'Et in terra pax'. Monteverdi's Venetian church music is indeed astonishingly varied, from the passionate, even at times desperate, pleas for intercession to the Blessed Virgin Mary to the intellectual and stately settings of psalms over ostinato basses. One can see why the Wardens of the confraternities would pay him considerable sums 'and thank him too'; why the Procurators of St Mark's insisted on his return from leave at Mantua or Parma to compose and conduct the music of their grand festivals; why the whole city 'ran to hear' when he made music anywhere in Venice; and why there was great mourning when he died in 1643. His music served the community at large in its religious devotions. Today it can do the same: for which of us does not feel the need of prayer, or wish to feel at one with his fellows in a communal act or – at times of despair want simply to utter a cry of anguish? Monteverdi does all these.

Conclusion

Monteverdi's madrigals and operas are usually thought of as the mainstay of his *oeuvre*: for was not the man a humanist, the disciple of Plato rather than of Jesus, the searcher for the 'moving of the affections', or exploiting man's emotions rather than seeking for divine rapture? All this is true, to a point; but the humanists were not anti-Christian, nor was Monteverdi's desire to convey human emotions exclusive. To see him, as one scholar has,[1] as a reluctant composer of church music is to misunderstand him. What is certainly true is that the nature of his religious feeling changed throughout his life – as it does with most people, especially those who live long. His early religious music, as student work, is hardly evidence. The Vespers, on the other hand, tell us a great deal of his search for stability and ecstasy in those awful years at Mantua after his wife had died: as indeed does the 'Gombert' Mass, with its continuous excitement achieved through intellectual means. His Venetian music comes after the crisis, when faith could once more be taken almost for granted. His letters reveal that he was still capable of being disturbed by events, his errant sons especially causing him worry; yet on the whole he seems to have been possessed of an enormous calm strength, shuddering only when he remembered those wild times in the service of the Gonzagas. His music reflects this, the great motets and psalm settings as much as any: for religion is one element in arriving at equilibrium.

That he was the last great Italian composer to leave us a substantial amount of fine church music is significant of changing times. The delights of the opera house soon seduced Monteverdi's pupil, Cavalli, who produced a good *Missa concertata*, some Vespers psalms and even a few excellent motets: but no real masterpiece to compare with his master's survives. Thereafter Italians, at least those who were successful, made religious music a secondary affair, and if there is good church music by Vivaldi, Galuppi, Jommelli and a few others, it must yield pride of place to their other activities. Nor do the

[1] L. Schrade, *Monteverdi: Creator of Modern Music* (London, 1951).

masterpieces of Rossini and Verdi disprove this rule: they are exceptional by any standards. It is no coincidence that the Vespers music published in 1610 and some of the works of the Venetian period seem to the public at large to presage the generally admitted greatness of Bach's Protestant declarations of faith. Monteverdi was born at the right time and suffered anguish enough to make his humanist principles spill over into Counter-Reformation fervour. It is the combination of the two which makes his music sound both modern and devout, and its continued revival assured today.

The Vespers: a note on editions and recordings

The various editions of the Vespers adopt such disparate attitudes to performing the music that the work frequently appears in quite different guises. It is therefore important to know which edition is being used, for it affects the whole attitude to its style.

The work was first rediscovered in the nineteenth century by the German scholar Carl von Winterfeld, who published part of it in his great book on Giovanni Gabrieli in 1834. It does not seem to have aroused much interest, however, until it was published complete in the Collected Edition of Monteverdi's works, edited by Gian Francesco Malipiero in 1932. This edition simply printed a score of the music as found in the original partbooks, without any interpretive comments, and although today this could act as the basis for a performance directed by a well-informed musicologist, it was clear that at the time most conductors required help to understand the conventions.

This help was provided by Hans F. Redlich, a musicologist who had written a thesis on Monteverdi's madrigals and was also a conductor at the Frankfurt Opera. His edition, first prepared for performances in Switzerland in the 1930s, was published in 1949 by Universal Edition, having been used in the meantime for performances at Morley College under Walter Goehr and Michael Tippett. His edition was based on wide reading of treatises on the performing methods of the early seventeenth century, most especially those described in Michael Praetorius' *Syntagma Musicum* Volume 3 (Wolfenbüttel, 1619), giving a distinctive German bias. Redlich missed out two of the psalms, considering the work not to have a natural unity. He doubled many of the voice parts in the psalms, divided up much of the music between solo and chorus (even in some places in the 'solo' motets), realised the continuo for a variety of instruments, and added ornaments, while at the same time putting in a vast number of expression and tempo markings. It thus emerged almost as an oratorio, certainly conceived on the same scale as Handelian performances, with a largish choir and a chamber orchestra, as well as solo singers. It is not too much to say that it appears in this guise as a romantic work; but the edition had the advantage that the Vespers in no sense could be seen as an 'antiquarian' work, but was one vibrating with emotion – even exaggeratedly so. It was recorded in the early 1950s by the Swabian Choral Society and Bach Orchestra conducted by H. Grischkat (Vox set PL 7902).

Shortly after the recording appeared, another by the London Singers and Oiseau Lyre Ensemble conducted by Anthony Lewis (OL 50021/2) was issued, using a manuscript version by the Germano–American scholar, Leo Schrade, which has never been published. Schrade saw the original as a straightforward source which could be used with little alteration. He did not remove psalms, and considered the motets as substitutes for antiphons. To judge from the recording, his editorial methods were not far from those commonly used today: but, by that time, Redlich's highly coloured version was considered both imaginative and scholarly and was much favoured by reviewers and performers alike.

The published version of Redlich's edition suffered from a large number of misprints (one scholar put them in the thousands!); and although its generally romantic attitude was followed in a highly flavoured version of Ghedini, often used in Italy, it was considered necessary to revise Redlich, a task done by the editor himself (Universal Edition, 1958) and, in effect, also by Walter Goehr who had conducted the version a number of times. Goehr's edition is distinctly more faithful to the original in many respects, it being possible to discover what is editorial and what original. But in the doublings of vocal lines, the general attitude to dynamic and tempo markings and the conception as a work for choir and orchestra it is generally the same as Redlich's, though the edition is certainly much more accurate. This version is often used today, though frequently modified by conductors.

These editions held sway until Denis Stevens put the cat among the pigeons with an entirely different edition (Novello, 1961).

Stevens considered that the motets were liturgically irrelevant and therefore missed them out, leaving only the five psalms, the hymn, and *Magnificat*. He provided plainsong antiphons to replace the motets, a procedure subsequently attacked in an influential article by the American scholar, Stephen Bonta, 'Liturgical problems in Monteverdi's Marian Vespers' (*Journal of the American Musicological Society*, Vol. xx, 1967), but nonetheless followed in some subsequent editions and recordings to the point where both plainsong *and* the motets are included. The actual text of the music was more closely followed, without doublings or other extraneous parts or elaborate interpretative markings. It was obviously conceived for smaller forces than former editions (and was thus recorded on VSL 11000-1 under the editor) and gained great currency, being both more convenient to perform – not needing a vast array of expensive soloists for the motets – and allowing more dynamic performances. Its omissions were, however, much criticised; the division of music between soloists and choir is not always effective and there are some minor and unnecessary alterations to Monteverdi's text.

Up to this time, there had been no question of a really 'authentic' performance, if only because several 'old' instruments , notably the cornetto, were considered unpractical. Thus all the editions had been to some extent adaptations. The edition made by the German conductor Gottfried Wolters (Möseler Verlag, Wolfenbüttel/Zürich 1966) is in effect an *Urtext*, giving a scholarly text with suggestions for orchestration in an appendix which can be ignored. The motets, all the psalms and the great *Magnificat* are included, with plainsong antiphons also in an appendix for use if desired. Emendations to Monteverdi's text (such as needed for *musica ficta*) are shown clearly as editorial. Thus it is possible to arrive at the original without trouble.

Whether this has been used for recordings is unclear, but the recent fashion has been to return to forces which are akin to those of the seventeenth century. Sometimes the peculiarities of the conditions at Mantua have not been understood. Thus the performance by the choir of King's College, Cambridge and the Early Music Consort (SLS 5064) suffers from the fact that the English choral tradition puts emphasis on the boys who sing the soprano parts and who outnumber the men on the lower lines in the choral pieces. The same is true to some extent of the recording by the Regensburg Choir and the Schneidt Ensemble (2723043) though this is interesting in using counter-tenors in place of women in the solo motets, a technique only made possible by adjustments of balance in making a recording, but which certainly gives a new idea of what the original sound, made by either castrati or falsettists, might have been.

A version by Jürgen Jürgens was published by Universal Edition in 1977 after having been in use for some years. Its free instrumental doublings and attitude to the divisions between solo and ripieno voices reveal the continuing though reduced influence of Redlich and Goehr, as does the recording by the Hamburg Monteverdi Choir and Concentus Musicus of Vienna (FA6 35045) which has some brilliant playing on single instruments offset by a surprisingly romantic slowness in the choral movements.

Lastly, a version with the *Lauda Jerusalem* and *Magnificat* transposed down to fit the ranges of the other movements was made by Andrew Parrott and given at the 'Proms' in 1979. Whether this will be published is unknown at this time. But it seems unlikely that there will ever be a final 'authentic' edition, either on paper or on record, and conductors have considerable freedom in producing their own versions.

Index of Works Discussed

(i) Monteverdi

(ii) others